# purity

# PURITY

LAWRENCE R. LUCAS

LUCAS COMPANY
MOSCOW

Lucas Company
Post Office Box 9245
Moscow, Idaho 83843
(208) 882-9504

© 2003 by Lawrence R. Lucas
All rights reserved,
including the right of reproduction
in whole or in part in any form.

Cover photo
© George D. Lepp/Corbis

Published 2003
Printed in the United States of America

Scripture taken from the HOLY BIBLE, NEW INTERNATIONAL VERSION®. Copyright © 1973, 1978, 1984 by International Bible Society. Used by permission of International Bible Society.

"NIV" and "NEW INTERNATIONAL VERSION" are trademarks registered in the United States Patent and Trademark office by International Bible Society

ISBN 0-9715916-1-X

*- To my younger brothers,
suiting up to fight
the good fight -*

*But among you there must not be even a hint of sexual immorality, or of any kind of impurity, or of greed...*

*For of this you can be sure: No immoral, impure or greedy person—such a man is an idolater— has any inheritance in the kingdom of Christ and of God.*

*Let no one deceive you with empty words, for because of such things God's wrath comes on those who are disobedient.*

Paul the Apostle
Letter to the Ephesians, chapter 5

*How can a young man keep his way pure? By living according to your word.*

*I have hidden your word in my heart that I might not sin against you.*

Psalm 119, verses 9 and 11

# CONTENTS

LET'S BEGIN ................................................. 11

WHERE ARE YOU? ....................................... 13

ASSURANCES AND DOUBTS ......................... 16

SEXUAL PURITY ........................................... 20

WHAT DO WE BELIEVE ABOUT GOD? ............. 21

SIN IS NOT INEVITABLE ................................. 22

THE LIE OF ENSLAVEMENT ............................ 25

FORGIVENESS ............................................. 27

TENNIS AND TEMPTATION ........................... 28

INVITED TEMPTATIONS ................................ 30

UNINVITED TEMPTATIONS ............................ 33

IN PRIVATE ................................................. 35

HOMOSEXUALITY ....................................... 36

WHERE IMPURITY LEADS .............................. 37

WHAT WILL YOU CHOOSE? .......................... 37

EPILOGUE- PASSAGES ON TEMPTATION ......... 40

    PATHS AND AFFECTIONS ......................... 41

      PROVISIONS ..................................... 47

APPENDIX–PSALMS TO CONSIDER ................. 51

# LET'S BEGIN

This small work is dedicated to you younger brothers, who have so much ahead of you: so much opportunity, so much promise, so much discovery and life. I pray you never outgrow being teachable; and that God, in His mercy, allows your humility to always outpace your gains in knowledge and strength.

It would be difficult to put into words the richness God intends for you, how utterly satisfying He is. Your sexuality is merely one aspect of this richness. Yes, sexuality is a gift from God, one of many. He thought it up without any help from us: puberty, the love between a man and a woman, intercourse... He created it all and then He gave it. And make no mistake, He intends you to enjoy it fully. Like His other gifts, though, you will enjoy it fully only when you enjoy it as He intends. This is clear in the Scriptures and it's clear in the lives and testimony of those who've gone before you. The question is, do you believe this? It's a matter of trust, you know.

When we're young, people pour advice on us. And here now in this booklet I'm dispensing advice, and asking you to please heed it; asking you to listen to me, to the Scriptures, and to the counsel of those who've gone ahead of you. It's a habit I hope you've not yet entirely abandoned. It seems to come under fire as we grow into our own abilities and understandings. Sometimes, too, those who give counsel seem unwilling to take it themselves. They want us to listen but don't want to listen in return. They want us to learn from them but are unwilling to learn from us. These things make it hard to listen, but they don't need to prevent it–the choice is yours. I urge you, please, don't let anything or anyone hinder you. Keep listening, keep taking things to heart, and remember: a man can grow in knowledge, size, and experience without growing in wisdom. You'll meet plenty who've done just that.

This is dedicated to the younger brothers, addressed to them really; but it aims at a much larger audience, an audience that includes men and women of all ages, an audience that includes you.

# WHERE ARE YOU?

Now because this booklet will likely fall into the hands of both the unsaved and the saved, it's important to cover some ground here at the beginning. First, for those of you who are not saved and know it, this counsel may be interesting, but you lack the freedom needed to implement it. Your relationship to sin is that of a slave to his master. You may find some success in resisting a few particular sins, but you are not dead to all of sin like a saved person. Despite appearances, sin has a grip on you, and when you stand before God on judgment day, as each one of us will, hell will be waiting to receive you.

This is a huge and immediate problem. We make the mistake of thinking, perhaps because it seems so far away, that it's much smaller than it is, or that there will be time to address it later. The opposite is true: in our worst nightmares we can not even start to imagine the size of this problem. And we only assume we'll have time; there's no guarantee. Any one of us might die before today ends. Then it will be too late.

Yet as big as this problem is it can be remedied here and now if you will simply repent and believe. That is, if you will decide to turn away from sin and ask God to save you, not because you deserve saving, but because Jesus died for your sins, was buried and then rose from the dead (just as God had promised beforehand in the Scriptures). This is a matter between you and God. You need to do business with Him on your own. He is quite willing to save you, but those are His terms: repent and believe. And when you have, openly tell others what you've done.

Let me elaborate: Jesus Christ, God's only begotten son, became a man and led a sinless life in order to pay men's debts, that is, redeem them. Which debts? The debts created by sin. You see, each of us has sinned, and sin has a cost associated with it, a cost that must be paid for each and every sin, without exception. That cost is death. One sin incurs the cost as surely as a thousand sins; one sin earns a man eternal separation from God in a place of unimaginable horror, with no hope of escape. *For the wages of sin is death...*(Romans 6:23).

Jesus, who never sinned, was crucified to bear that penalty in our place, so that we could be spared the punishment we've earned for ourselves. But that's not the end– three days after He was killed and buried He rose from the dead. Death couldn't hold Him and He's alive today. Because of all this, all that He did, we can be forgiven and have eternal life; that is, we can know Him, know God.

Since the penalty has already been paid, God can offer each of us forgiveness and life everlasting as a gift. The gift part is important though, because nothing you have done or ever will do can earn you this forgiveness. And the gift is accepted by faith, which means a man must decide to trust Christ's payment rather than any good deed, or word, or intention he might be able to come up with on his own. You see, nothing you can ever do will count toward payment of this debt.

Further, you must transact this deal with God on your own, this deal to trust Him for the gift. No one can do it for you. But bear in mind, you cannot turn to Him to do business without simultaneously turning away from sin. If you're determined to hold on to some sins, or if you don't think you really need saving (because after all, you know people far worse than you) there will be no deal.

These are His terms. He's the one you sinned against. He's the one who will judge you on the last day. And He's the one who, at a staggering cost to Himself, has provided this one, single opportunity for forgiveness. None of us are in a position to dicker over these terms.

# ASSURANCES AND DOUBTS

Now, back to the rest of you. Each of you falls into one of three categories: saved and sure of it, saved and doubting it, and unsaved but thinking you are. What I'm going to cover next is for the benefit of those in the last two categories. It has to do with the evidences in a person's life that they have been saved. If these traits describe you, you're saved. Quit doubting. If these don't describe you, you're not saved. It doesn't matter whether you're going to church, leading Bible studies, even doing evangelism: you are not saved. Please do not be fooled. But again, if you conclude you are not saved, the problem can be remedied immediately. See the preceding paragraphs.

Here's what the Bible says about the evidence in a person's life that they are saved:

First, a saved person has a love for the brethren, that is, other Christians. In his first letter, the Apostle John writes, *"We know that we have passed from death to life, because we love our brothers."* (1 John 3:14) A Christian's love for other Christians (his brothers and sisters in Christ) is intended to serve as an assurance to him that he has passed from death to life, that is, that he has been saved. I believe one of the main ways this shows up in our lives is in who we want to be with, who we feel at home with, and on the other hand, who we feel out of place with.

A Christian is at home with other Christians; they are the company he seeks out. This isn't to say Christians should be isolated from others, but they sense a fundamental difference when they're with unsaved people. With other Christians they share Christ dwelling within them. With non-Christians they don't. That's my understanding of how this love, in part, plays out.

Let me digress for a moment. Whenever you hear me, or someone else, say, "that's my opinion" or "that's how I understand or interpret it", remember this: we may be wrong. Whenever anyone moves beyond the actual words of the Bible, they introduce the possibility of error. This does not mean they *are* wrong, but rather that the possibility has been introduced. You won't always get this impression by listening because some people tend to present their views quite forcefully. It's as though they've forgotten that while the Bible is infallible, they are not. Forcefulness, like volume, doesn't change this. So be careful what you believe. Learn to distinguish fact from opinion. Learn to verify what you're taught. All good teachers will encourage you to do the same. They recognize that we can rely on what's actually stated in the Bible, and that anything else may or may not be true.

Now regarding this love of the brothers, it is not to be confused with feeling at home in a denomination. The real thing comes from God and operates His way. It is a love for other Christians, regardless of where they go to church. A Christian isn't someone who goes to the Nazarene Church or Baptist Church, loves other Nazarenes or Baptists, but not other Christians. A Christian loves Christians. We can feel quite at home in a denomination, especially one with a strong sense of community, and still not love other Christians. That's not love of the brethren, it's love of the other club members. This is one of the problems with a strong sense of denominational belonging or pride: it can give false assurance to someone who desperately needs to be saved.

The second evidence of being saved is the discipline of God in our lives. In Hebrews we're told, *"...My son, do not make light of the Lord's discipline, and do not lose heart when he rebukes you, because the Lord disciplines those he loves, and he punishes everyone he accepts as a son. Endure hardship as discipline; God is treating you as sons. For what son is not disciplined by his father? If you are not disciplined (and everyone undergoes discipline), then you are illegitimate children and not true sons."* (Hebrews 12:5-8) When a man gets saved, he is adopted by God as a son. He is forgiven for all the sins he has committed in the past, no matter how mean or gross. And because all his sins are forgiven, including the giant ones, they don't bother him any longer. However, once saved, if he now sins, even a small unkind word that likely wouldn't have bothered him before, he feels awful. It's as though he's developed a heightened sensitivity to sin. The big sins from the past don't bother him, but new sins do. Why? Because now he's being disciplined by God. God is treating him as a son. And God does not let His sons get away with sin. He disciplines them, and when He does it's unpleasant.

The third evidence is found in 1 Corinthians. There the apostle Paul writes, to Christians, *"We have not received the spirit of the world but the Spirit who is from God, that we may understand what God has freely given us...The man without the Spirit does not accept the things that come from the Spirit of God, for they are foolishness to him, and he cannot understand them, because they are spiritually discerned."* (1 Corinthians 2:12,14) God has given His Spirit to each saved person, in part to help us understand. Spiritual things make no sense to unspiritual men, they seem foolish to them. But to spiritual men, men to whom the Spirit of God has been given, spiritual things make wonderful sense. So when a man gets saved his understanding changes. For instance, the things written in the Bible, which is a spiritual book filled with spiritual things, start to make all kinds of sense–far more sense than they ever did before.

Now there are other evidences, and I don't mean to downplay their importance, but I think these three will give you a pretty good indication of where you stand. If these three describe your life, quit doubting. If they don't, you have cause to doubt.

What follows then is written to Christians: men and women saved by Christ.

# SEXUAL PURITY

There is only one way for a saved person to maintain sexual purity: consistently choose not to sin.

Wait, you were expecting more. Well there isn't any more. It really is that simple. It always will be. And that's both wonderful and sobering. It's wonderful because it's so clean and basic. It requires no advanced theological training, no special circumstances, no secret formula. It has already been provided for in the atoning death and resurrection of Jesus Christ and in the faithfulness of God, who never changes, who never even wavers.

However, it's sobering as well, because of what it implies. You see, each sin of impurity is the result of a choice to sin, not some irresistible temptation or overpowering drive, but a choice. Problems arise when we're fooled into believing differently, which we all too readily are.

We have an enemy that wars against us, and he could probably get by with just one weapon–deceit. We know he's a liar; in fact Jesus calls him the father of lies. Even so, he hasn't had to add to his arsenal because the same weapon has worked for thousands of years. We are not as clever as we might think.

So if lies are being used against us, let's dispel them with the truth.

# WHAT DO WE BELIEVE ABOUT GOD?

In his second letter, the apostle Peter writes this about God: *"His divine power has given us everything we need for life and godliness through our knowledge of him who called us by his own glory and goodness. Through these he has given us his very great and precious promises, so that through them you may participate in the divine nature and escape the corruption in the world caused by evil desires."* (II Peter 1: 3-4)

There are a couple of things to notice here: first, the power needed for life and godliness has already been given.

The verb "given" is in the past tense. It's a transaction completed for each of us when we're saved. Second, God has also given us promises. Why? To enable us to participate in the divine nature and escape the corruption caused by evil desires. Now ask yourself this: What are the two possible responses to promises?

Well, we can choose to believe them or doubt them. That is, we can choose to trust the person making the promises or to not trust him. The "him", in this case, is God.

Just how then are we supposed to put these promises to use? Well, by relying on them. By believing them in spite of what we feel like, what the circumstances look like, or what past history indicates. We use God's promises by simply deciding to trust the one who made them. The choice is always ours and it's always the same: to trust or distrust God.

# SIN IS NOT INEVITABLE

Now one of the promises God has made to the saved is found in Paul's first letter to the Corinthians:
*No temptation has seized you except what is common to man. And God is faithful; he will not let you be tempted beyond*

*what you can bear.  But when you are tempted, he will also provide a way out so that you can stand up under it.*
(I Corinthians 10:13)

This passage is so clear that it seems unnecessary to comment on it; but it's crucial too, so in case you missed any part of the point:  God promises here to *never* let you be tempted beyond what you can bear.  It doesn't matter how powerful the temptation seems, you can bear it, you need not fall.  Furthermore, He will *always* provide a way out so that you can stand up under it.

Wait a minute, you say.  You don't know how hard it is not to sin when I'm tempted.  Well, that may or may not be true, I may not know.  God however does know; and He has clearly promised to always provide you a way out and to never let you be tempted beyond what you can bear.  Those are the facts.  What you do with them is critical.

Should you choose to believe them, you will find them wonderfully true.  Sin's illusory grasp will evaporate.  Should you choose to not believe, and let's be clear, this is a choice to not trust God, you're unlikely to escape the corruption in the world caused by evil desires.

Wait a minute, you say.  Every Christian I know falls to temptation.  Well, that may be.  God's point here is that they don't have to, ever.  They could choose not to.  Whenever they have been tempted He has always, without fail, provided them a way of escape. He has never let them be tempted beyond what they could bear. And because He is faithful, this will always be the case. They have a choice and so do you: believe God or don't. If you choose not to, the reason hardly matters. You'll want to think it does, but it really doesn't.

Wait a minute. Other Christians have told me it's unrealistic to expect to never fall to temptation again for the rest of my life. Have they now? Well, you have a choice then, don't you; and unfortunately they can't decide for you. Will you believe God or not? It's a choice you will need to make yourself. Besides, thinking about every temptation for the rest of your life is just a trick to make God's provision seem impossible. It makes far more sense to think about the *next* temptation you'll face, whatever it might be. Do you believe God will provide a means of escape from that next one?

Let me ask just this: why do you suppose that in the middle of this promise God says, "*...And God is faithful;...*" Why do you think He says that just there?

No, sin is not inevitable. And believing otherwise is believing a lie.

# THE LIE OF ENSLAVEMENT

Unsaved people are slaves to sin. Christians are not. They've been set free. Sin can't hold them against their will. Yet sometimes it seems Christians enter into a voluntary enslavement by persisting in a sin. I say voluntary because they're free to walk away from any such entanglement whenever they like. This is a basic difference between a Christian and an unsaved person. But don't take my word for it, read the sixth chapter of Paul's letter to the Romans.

Now in saying this, I need to emphasize something. The passage I just referred to is clear about our prior enslavement and our current freedom. The idea of temporary enslavement, however, is less clear. My interpretation may be wrong. My only purpose in bringing it up is this: sometimes it seems to Christians that they are being held captive by a sin, and perhaps what they're feeling is this voluntary enslavement. Either way, whether temporary enslavement is possible or not, a Christian can put it off and walk away any time he pleases. If he's in a cell, the door is unlocked.

Sometimes Christians struggle against sin as though their freedom had never been bought, as though the outcome hinged on their strength rather than what Christ has already done. It's a great tactic for the enemy. In fact, it's the only tactic he has left. The fight is over; the prisoners have already been set free. All the enemy can do is trick a Christian into thinking otherwise.

One thing you should be gathering here is the importance of knowing the truth. Without truth, you're a sucker for any halfway believable lie that shows up on the doorstep. So how do you go about knowing the truth? Of course, you read your Bible, regularly. You pay attention to what you read. You don't re-word it or restrict its meaning to fit your experience because you think something it promises or commands is impossible. With God all things are possible. You ask God to please, please, please give you understanding, and wisdom, because you don't want to be a sucker. You don't want whoever's married to you to be married to a sucker. And when you're older and have children looking up to you, you don't want them to be depending on a sucker.

You need to go after the truth and hang onto it for dear life, because the truth is what's going to get attacked.

# FORGIVENESS

Remember earlier I said that when you get saved all the sins you had ever committed were forgiven? Well, what if you sin afterwards, after you've been saved? That's easy, you simply confess the sin to God, that is you tell God you were wrong, no excuses. He already knows you were wrong so what you're doing is simply agreeing with Him about the nature of the thought, word, or deed: it was sin. And when you confess, He will forgive you.

If, however, you don't confess your sins, you'll be miserable; because God will discipline you, and as we covered earlier, discipline is unpleasant. Look at David in the first five verses of Psalm 32 or the first few verses of Psalm 38. Go ahead, look now. You might as well start the habit of checking things out for yourself to see what's true. I'll put them in the back of this booklet in case you don't have a Bible handy.

Do you see why David is hurting? It's because of his sin. The only cure is for him to own up to it. And if you look at the first four verses of Psalm 51 you'll see a perfect example of what that owning up (confession) looks like. David doesn't try to make himself look better, he doesn't try to make excuses, he doesn't try to shift the blame to someone else or say it was the circumstances. He simply agrees with

God. He then goes on to get another important thing right: the sin was against God.

When the apostle John wrote the first of his three letters in the New Testament, he said this about God,
*If we confess our sins, he is faithful and just and will forgive us our sins and purify us from all unrighteousness.* (I John 1:9)

That's another one of those promises we rely on. Your feelings may say God hasn't forgiven you, but the truth is otherwise.

# TENNIS AND TEMPTATION

I heard an analogy once that resisting temptation is like a tennis match. When a temptation crosses the net into our court, our job is to hit it back out. We don't pick it up and look at it. We don't play around with it. We knock it back out of our court. That seems especially suited to impure thoughts. When one comes over the net, you need to get rid of it. If you let it hang around you'll sin.

There are a couple of related thoughts I need to develop here. The first is this: when an impure thought pops into your mind uninvited, it's not sin. It's temptation looking to become sin. In the book of James this process of temptation becoming sin is discussed in the first chapter. Now I point this out because it can become quite discouraging when we, wanting to avoid sin, confuse it with temptation. Again, it's a great trick of the enemy to lob a temptation into our court and then accuse us of having sinned. And again, knowing the truth protects us (remember, no suckers).

The other thought is this: our minds aren't supposed to just sit vacant waiting for something to pop in. We're called on to actively use them, to set them *on things above, not on earthly things.* (Colossians 3:2), to think about *"whatever is true, whatever is noble...right...pure..."* (Philippians 4:8). We use them to pray (that is, talk to God), to think through what we've read in the Bible, to ask God questions about what we've read or heard, to thank Him for what He's done for us, and for others...

Now all these things are there in the text. You'll come across them, *if you read God's Word.* But the point is this: when we actively fill our thoughts with good things, there's not as much room for bad. It's simple really. And in a way it's a reflection of a larger aspect of our lives with Christ: we aren't intended to always be on the defensive, always struggling to avoid sin. Rather, we're to occupy ourselves with the offensive: doing good, encouraging others, helping where we see needs, practicing kindness, praying, giving thanks... In other words, when we decide we're going to take up the offense spiritually, we find we're no longer preoccupied with defense, and further, we don't need to be.

# INVITED TEMPTATIONS

### CIRCUMSTANCES

God has given us vast freedom in arranging our circumstances. We can either avoid a temptation or invite it. That is, we can either stack the deck in our favor or to our disadvantage. Let me explain.

Making yourself available to pornography, either in print, on television or on the Internet stacks the deck against you, especially in private settings where you have reason to believe your sin will go undetected. Likewise, an unmarried man and woman have the deck stacked against them when they spend time alone together in a house or bedroom.

None of this is profound. It's not some deep, hidden mystery. It's simply the result of thinking about how temptation works. Each of us could, with little difficulty, describe circumstances that would work against us, in which we'd likely be tempted. We need look no farther than where we've been regularly tempted in the past. Those are circumstances we should stay away from. And the decision to stay away should be made in advance.

Bad circumstances can be easily avoided. That's not the problem. Sure, it takes some attentiveness. It takes some thought. But more than that it takes resolve; because ultimately the decision to stay away from tempting circumstances is just that, a decision, like the decision to not sin. Likewise, the decision to flirt with temptation, to remain in its vicinity rather than flee, is a conscious choice. God isn't fooled. He knows.

## COMPANY

Companions can be a source of temptation: people who want to go places you shouldn't go, do things you shouldn't do, watch movies you shouldn't watch, talk about things you shouldn't talk about. Sometimes these companions are Christians, sometimes they only think they are. Avoid such people.

They may be in a Bible study, or church, or other small group with you. If so, the decision to quit socializing with them could be awkward. You will likely be accused of being legalistic, or self-righteous, or something else. Expect consequences, and remember, you're being asked to choose between God and man, and you're choosing God. Don't get lured into the, "I don't want to hurt their feelings" trap. Just stay away.

It's possible that your decision to avoid temptation will serve as a wake up call to your friend. If he's a Christian this could be just what he's needed. It might prompt him to make the same choices you've made. This would be a joyful outcome, because among other benefits, you gain a genuine friend, who can encourage and reinforce your own resolve. But remember, this outcome doesn't happen without the initial decision on your part; and you need to stick with your decision, whatever the outcome.

## CONDITIONING

Our lifestyle can help or hinder us. For instance, laziness is a bad habit. It caters to a lack of self-control. Diligence, on the other hand, is a good habit. It first develops and then nourishes self-control, which in turn helps us consistently make good decisions and then hold to them.

Being considerate of others is a good practice. It prompts us to feed the hungry and give drink to the thirsty. It helps us notice those needs in the first place. It's a sign of maturity. It takes the offensive spiritually.

Idle time and its child, boredom, are invitations to sin. Television is no remedy, and I have doubts about other amusements that involve staring at a screen. Work, on the other hand, *is* a remedy to boredom, so is pursuing an interest or hobby.

Spiritual malnutrition lowers our resistance (as does unconfessed sin). How does someone become malnourished? By not taking in enough spiritual nutrients, i.e. not taking in God's word, not participating in fellowship with other Christians, not talking to God (prayer), not expressing gratitude to God or worshipping Him.

Finally, I suspect that inadequate sleep and poor diet can also work against us.

# UNINVITED TEMPTATIONS

## IMMODESTY

Because men are so readily tempted by what they see, how a woman dresses in their company is important. Men all understand this, as do most women. Those who don't are either naïve or foolish, they betray a fundamental ignorance of men. Yet even those who understand tend to underestimate the strength of the temptation they present when they dress immodestly.

What's immodest? Well, the easiest way for a woman to know is to ask. Who to ask? Start with other women, especially men's wives and mothers. They have a vested interest in their husbands' and sons' spiritual well being. Actually, all saved people have a vested interest in each other's spiritual condition, but people with these family relationships are less likely to forget theirs.

I mentioned above that some women don't understand how readily men can be tempted. Their flaw, if not sin, is thoughtlessness. They ignore God's admonition: *Each of you should look not only to your own interests, but also to the interests of others.* (Philippians 2:4)

The more sinister problem is posed by women who understand all too well, who deliberately dress to appeal to men's sexual appetites. In the Gospel of Luke Jesus says, " *'Things that cause people to sin are bound to come, but woe to that person through whom they come. It would be better for him to be thrown into the sea with a millstone tied around his neck than for him to cause one of these little ones to sin.'"* (Luke 17:1-2) We sometimes act as if He were joking, as if He were merely being melodramatic.

When a woman tries to get attention in this way she usually does, but it's all the wrong kind.

Women, however, are not the only guilty parties to this. Men are equally at fault when they encourage immodesty, when they repeatedly send the message, "If you want my attention, earn it by looking sexy, because I'm more interested in looks than godliness, helpfulness, kindness, faithfulness, gentleness..." In other words, "I'm more interested in how you *look* than how you *are*, and because I've got it all wrong I'd like you to get it wrong too."

One of the worst things that can happen to a man who wants a sexually provocative wife is to get his wish.

# IN PRIVATE

Masturbation leads to sinful desires and feeds on sinful imaginings. Over time it leads farther and farther down into depravity as the imaginings worsen, and in this sense it provides a built-in warning, an ever-steepening slide downward. Pay attention to the warning. Consider where this is leading. Death is waiting.

# HOMOSEXUALITY

There's a popular myth gaining wide acceptance. It holds that people are born homosexuals. It's how they're wired. The myth, lie really, is then followed by some faulty reasoning to draw two utterly false conclusions: first, homosexuality must be acceptable because God made people that way; and second, it's useless to resist any such urges.

The truth is, people choose to commit homosexual acts, just as someone might choose to lie, or steal or murder. It's true that some people are never tempted to commit homosexuality, just as some are never tempted to lie, others never to steal and still others never to murder. The man who's tempted to lie is no more a liar than the man who's tempted to steal is a thief. It's the man who tells lies that is a liar and the man who steals that is a thief. Likewise, it's the man or woman who chooses to live as a homosexual, engaging in homosexual acts, that is a homosexual.

The temptation to homosexuality means nothing. It no more keeps someone from a godly, delightful, heterosexual life than a craving to eat too much pizza does. What matters is how we respond to temptation. Furthermore, a fall to this temptation, like any other sin, can be repented of, in which case it will be forgiven, and the Christian will be left with a fresh, clean start.

# WHERE IMPURITY LEADS

God is pretty clear about something: the sexually immoral will not inherit the kingdom of God (I Corinthians 6:9). But before that final judgment, other consequences will likely appear: expulsion from the company of the saints, betrayal and divorce, breaking the hearts of those who love you, shame, increasing depravity, possibly disease, even prison.

No clear thinking person would choose these outcomes all at once. It would be ridiculous. Rather, these are *eased* into. They're chosen one sin at a time, when it seems much less harmful and these costs seem so far removed they're practically invisible.

# WHAT WILL YOU CHOOSE?

The decision for purity is made over and over again, day after day. It's a decision to obey God, and it's a decision to trust Him as well, to believe what He says. By His grace you were first saved, and it was through believing

Him; that's how you escaped punishment and were granted life everlasting. Are you willing to trust Him with eternity but not with today?

God says He has something good intended for you. He says it is beyond your ability to imagine. Could it be that you know more than He does? More about pleasure? More about pain? More about what's of value? More about the costs of things? "No!" we say; but the real answer is seen in how we live.

Oh, but it takes faith, it takes a decision to trust; like the decision David made the moment before he walked out alone to face that giant Philistine; like the decisions Joseph made over and over as Potiphar's wife was trying to seduce him. We look back and these men seem larger than life. But they weren't really any bigger than you. It was who they trusted that made them seem big, because as big as they trusted, He never failed them, He had given His word. And for Him nothing was impossible–and still, nothing is. No, these weren't big men, they were just plain men trusting a big God, plain men who day after day had chosen to trust, so that when the big moments came, to them it was just one more decision. It didn't matter that sometimes the issue was being saved from enemies and at others times it was deciding to believe what God said about rewards and consequences. The trust was all part of the same fabric.

God invites you to: *Taste and see that the Lord is good.* (Psalm 34:8) Go ahead, see for yourself. He wants you to. And no one can do this for you.

Nor can anyone fully explain what it's like to know God, how utterly satisfying He is. Words simply fail. But we can perhaps get some idea by considering what Solomon said about wisdom. King Solomon, in the midst of all that he had accomplished, all that he owned and all that he knew, said this about wisdom: *"Nothing you desire can compare with her."* (Proverbs 3:15) No possession, no pleasure (sexual or otherwise), no amount of fame or esteem, nothing, can compare with wisdom. And wisdom, bear in mind, is merely *one* of the *gifts* of God–what must the *giver* of such gifts be like? Taste and see. If you draw near to Him, He has promised to draw near to you. How do you draw near? Why not ask Him? He wants to show you. He wants you to know.

There is only one way for a saved person to maintain sexual purity: consistently choose not to sin; for *"...God is faithful; he will not let you be tempted beyond what you can bear. But when you are tempted, he will also provide a way out so that you can stand up under it."* (1 Corinthians 10:13)

# EPILOGUE

## PASSAGES ON TEMPTATION

This epilogue draws from several passages in the Bible where temptation is discussed. There are many others not included. And there are still more which, while they don't *explicitly* mention temptation, contribute to our understanding of the subject. So the selection here is limited, best to be considered an introduction or supplement rather than a thorough treatment. Now when I say "introduction or supplement", I've chosen those words carefully. They are meant to encourage further study on your own, which will happen if you get serious about acquiring wisdom. God wants us to grow in wisdom and understanding; any hold-ups are at our end.

Further, to keep this brief I've pared down the amount of actual Bible text included, sometimes to a single verse, sometimes to a small cluster. This is common practice in writing that refers to the Scriptures (sometimes only the location of a verse is given). But keep in mind that it is always a good idea to look up verses when they're presented, so that you can see them in their context. Why? because the Bible is often misunderstood by those who quote it, sometimes intentionally, and you should learn to verify its usage. Reading verses in their context, that is, reading them as part of the surrounding verses, as part of the larger thought being developed, as part of the chapter or book they occur in, *clarifies* their meaning. Context both enlightens and protects.

That said, I want to begin by reminding you of a verse from the earlier discussion. Please don't lose sight of it in what follows.

> *No temptation has seized you except what is common to man...God is faithful; he will not let you be tempted beyond what you can bear. But when you are tempted, he will also provide a way out so that you can stand up under it.*
>
> (I Corinthians 10:13)

## PATHS AND AFFECTIONS

In the first nine chapters of Proverbs, God presents the image of a father speaking to his child. It portrays a man entrusting important things he has learned to his son. Now fathers learn in many ways, from many sources. Some lessons they pay dearly for, others cost them nothing. They learn from their own mistakes and from the mistakes of others. They learn from success as well as failure, at work as well as play. Some things they learned when they were still children, long before they ever thought of being fathers. The wisest among them *search* for wisdom, they seek it out - understanding is important to them. And God repays their efforts.

In Proverbs we see a father who knows his son will have to make choices of his own. So he is trying to prepare his son, urging him to heed his counsel and benefit. He wants his son to realize the gravity of these matters, to understand what it costs when a man gets them wrong, and to appreciate the benefits that follow getting them right. Love for his son is what drives the conversation. And I suspect that's a part of why God chose this image of a father and son to instruct us here in Proverbs, so that we too will grasp the importance of these matters. He is, after all, our father; and He loves us with a father's love. God wants us to get things right, for our sake.

It's in the course of this advice, spanning several chapters, that temptation is discussed. The subject is not merely touched on. It's visited again and again. Nor is the advice vague. It is frank and descriptive. Let's listen in and see what we can learn.

> *My son, if sinners entice you, do not give in to them...*
> *do not go along with them, do not set foot on their paths;*
>
> (Proverbs 1:10, 15)

Sometimes temptation comes as an invitation from others. Notice here *how* sinners entice, they try to talk us into joining them, into going along. Part of their appeal is the invitation to be included in their group, to be *with* them. Most of us have a desire to belong. We don't want to be left out. And because we don't want to be excluded we're tempted to go along, just a bit perhaps. And we might rationalize that, after all, we can withdraw before the actual sinning starts.

Not so, we're warned. Do not go along. Do not set a single foot on their path.

Staying off the wrong path recurs in chapter 4, with the added warning to turn away from it, to leave the vicinity:

> *Do not set foot on the path of the wicked or walk in the way of evil men.*
> *Avoid it, do not travel on it; turn from it and go on your way.*
> (Proverbs 4:14-15)

I don't think we can be too simple in understanding this. We're to keep a distance between us, and that which leads to sin.

Consider this from Proverbs 5, talking about the adulteress:

> *Keep to a path far from her; do not go near the door of her house,*
>
> (Proverbs 5:8)

This isn't theoretical; it's practical. It contains a principle, but we obey it literally as well. It's geography, but not only geography. And it's not only about staying away from bad paths, it's about choosing and then staying on the right one. In chapter 2 this father assures his son that if he heeds his commands and inclines his ear to wisdom, searching for it as for hidden treasure, then:

> *... you will walk in ways of good men and keep to the paths of the righteous.*
>
> (Proverbs 2:20)

What we choose here is critical, and we can't avoid the decision. Wandering along where the currents take us is as much a decision as choosing the wrong or right path, and following the current, going with the flow, usually turns out to be a bad decision. We need to give thought to our ways.

So what is a path? Well it seems to take in not just where we go, but how we fill our time, what we think about, and as a result what we talk about. I think it also includes interests we cultivate, desires we feed, and what we then decide to seek. It involves who our companions will be and who we'll risk running into along the way. And these paths which we choose day to day, when added up, will be the course of our *lives*, and they'll betray who or what was precious to us, who or what our hearts were set on.

So Proverbs tells us in the midst of these first nine chapters, where temptation is so frequently discussed:

> *Above all else, guard your heart, for it is the wellspring of life.*
> (Proverbs 4:23)

You see, we can open a door to temptation by what we desire, that is, what we hold dear in our hearts. In Proverbs 6 and 7 we see the two sides of this: first, in what we must keep ourselves from desiring and then in what we must desire instead.

> *Do not lust in your heart after her (the immoral woman) beauty or let her captivate you with her eyes,*
> *Can a man scoop fire into his lap without his clothes being burned?*
> (Proverbs 6:25-28)

> *My son, keep my words and store up my commands within you.*
> *Keep my commands and you will live;*

> *guard my teachings as the apple of your eye.*
> *Bind them on your fingers; write them on the tablet of your heart.*
> *Say to wisdom, "You are my sister," and call understanding your kinsman;*
> *they will keep you from the adulteress... with her seductive words.*
>
> (Proverbs 7:1-5)

It's a mistake to think that desire just grows without any participation on our part. It's linked to what we pursue, what we seek. In order to thrive desires must be fed, and we each choose which desires we're going to feed. But it's not enough to quit feeding sinful desires, we're told to actively cultivate godly ones (including the desire for God himself). It's no coincidence that our wants (desires) are repeatedly found in Bible passages dealing with temptation. Let's consider some New Testament verses.

> *People who want to get rich fall into temptation and a trap and into many foolish and harmful desires that plunge men into ruin and destruction. For the love of money is a root of all kinds of evil... But you, man of God, flee from all this, and pursue righteousness, godliness, faith, love, endurance and gentleness.*
>
> (1 Timothy 6:9-12)

People who want to get rich fall into temptation. And people who want to be popular, admired, or famous fall into temptation. We will invariably seek what we desire, what we've set our hearts on. In his first letter, the Apostle John warns:

> *Do not love the world or anything in the world. If anyone loves the world, the love of the Father is not in him. For everything in the world—the cravings of sinful man, the lust of his eyes and the boasting of what he has and does—comes not from the Father but from the world.*
>
> (1 John 2:15-16)

Pay attention. Guard your heart.


## PROVISIONS

There are just a couple more passages I'd like to bring to your attention regarding temptation. The first is taken from the Apostle Paul's letter to the Christians in Ephesus. He's near the end of a long letter when he brings up the subject of spiritual warfare. Here's what he writes to the Ephesians:

> *Finally, be strong in the Lord and in his mighty power. Put on the full armor of*

> *God so that you can take your stand against the devil's schemes. For our struggle is not against flesh and blood, but against the rulers, against the authorities, against the powers of this dark world and against the spiritual forces of evil in the heavenly realms. Therefore put on the full armor of God, so that when the day of evil comes, you may be able to stand your ground, and after you have done everything, to stand.*
>
> (Ephesians 6:10-13)

What can we learn here? In part, we 're told that these Christians are in a war. It's the same war Paul is in. But it's not against flesh and blood. Further, we learn that God has made provision for them. He's given them full armor and twice ordered them to put on *all* of it. He also orders them to be strong in Him. The verses following these deserve careful study, which I'll leave to you. They describe the armor, order the Christians to prayer, tell them to be alert, and then once more order them to prayer. *All* of this is important. But for purposes of this appendix, I merely want to point out that a war is going on, the enemy is unseen, and God has provided armor, His power and explicit instructions.

So how do you "be strong in the Lord"? Well, I have some thoughts on it but it would be best for you to ask Him. Likewise, if you don't understand how to use the armor or how to put it on, ask Him. After all it's His power and it's His armor, and He is very interested in you understanding. He knows you (better than you know yourself), and He knows the best way of getting through to you. So ask Him your questions. Make your requests to Him. Then thank Him and wait on Him, that is, trust Him to answer. Other Christians may shed great light on this for you. And God may use them to answer your "how?" questions. This is good. In a way though, it's seems rather like dancing a waltz. Many people can describe the steps for you, but it's God you'll be on the dance floor with, He'll be the one leading. Your job is to follow. So be strong in the Lord, and put your armor on.

In Hebrews there's more about God's provision for us when we're tempted.

> *For we do not have a high priest who is unable to sympathize with our weaknesses, but we have one who has been tempted in every way, just as we are—yet was without sin. Let us then approach the throne of grace with confidence, so that we may receive mercy and find grace to help us in our time of need.*
>
> (Hebrews 4:15-16)

The high priest being referred to here is Christ. He is able to sympathize with our weaknesses, He has been tempted in every way we are, and He didn't sin. Knowing this we're supposed to get help in our time of need. Specifically, we're to get mercy and grace, at the throne of grace, which we can approach with confidence.

You might be wondering where this throne of grace is. Again, I recommend asking God. Wherever it is, we know it's within reach. When I asked, it didn't matter to me *where* it was; I just needed Him to train my feet to run there. He and I both know that I need Him to lead me there, where He waits, ready to help. But in asking God remember, we're responding to invitations or exhortations He has already patiently laid out in His Word, which He wants us to pay attention to. He always welcomes our asking, but He doesn't want us to ignore the counsel He's already given. Most often, we will receive our answers as we (and *if* we) read the Bible.

# APPENDIX

## PSALMS TO CONSIDER

### PSALM 32:1-5

*Blessed is he whose transgressions*
*    are forgiven,*
*        whose sins are covered.*
*Blessed is the man whose sin the Lord*
*    does not count against him*
*        and in whose spirit is no deceit.*
*When I kept silent, my bones wasted away*
*    through my groaning all day long.*
*For day and night your hand*
*    was heavy upon me;*
*        my strength was sapped*
*            as in the heat of summer.  Selah*
*Then I acknowledged my sin to you*
*    and did not cover up my iniquity.*
*I said, "I will confess my transgressions*
*    to the Lord"—*
*and you forgave the guilt of my sin.  Selah*

## PSALM 38:1-8

*O Lord, do not rebuke me in your anger*
  *or discipline me in your wrath.*
*For your arrows have pierced me,*
  *and your hand has come down*
    *upon me.*
*Because of your wrath there is no*
  *health in my body;*
      *my bones have no soundness*
        *because of my sin.*
*My guilt has overwhelmed me*
  *like a burden too heavy to bear.*
*My wounds fester and are loathsome*
  *because of my sinful folly.*
*I am bowed down and brought very low;*
  *all day long I go about mourning.*
*My back is filled with searing pain;*
  *there is no health in my body.*
*I am feeble and utterly crushed;*
  *I groan in anguish of heart.*

## PSALM 51:1-4

*Have mercy on me, O God,*
*according to your unfailing love;*
*according to your great compassion*
*blot out my transgressions.*
*Wash away all my iniquity*
*and cleanse me from my sin.*
*For I know my transgressions,*
*and my sin is always before me.*
*Against you, you only, have I sinned*
*and done what is evil in your sight,*
*so that you are proved right when you*
*speak and justified when you judge.*